The Kids' Career Library™

A Day in the Life of a
Sculptor

Liza N. Burby

The Rosen Publishing Group's
PowerKids Press™
New York

Many thanks to David Haussler of Fort Salonga for his help with this book.

Published in 1999 by The Rosen Publishing Group, Inc.
29 East 21st Street, New York, NY 10010

First Edition

Book Design: Erin McKenna

Photo Illustrations: All photo illustrations by Christine Innamorato.

Burby, Liza N.
     A day in the life of a sculptor / by Liza N. Burby.
        p.   cm. — (The kids' career library)
     Includes index.
     Summary: Describes how a sculptor creates a metal seahorse.
     ISBN 0-8239-5305-X
     1. Haussler, David—Psychology—Juvenile literature. 2. Sculpture—Technique—Juvenile literature.
     [1. Sculpture. 2. Sculptors. 3. Occupations.] I. Title. II. Series.
     NB237.H365B87 1998
     730' .92—dc21
                                                            98-4608
                                                              CIP
                                                              AC

Manufactured in the United States of America

Contents

In David's Studio

David Haussler is an artist and a **sculptor** (SKULP-ter). Every weekend he goes to his **studio** (STOO-dee-oh) inside his barn. Here, he creates pieces of art called **sculptures** (SKULP-sherz). Some are made of **plaster** (PLAS-ter). Some are made of clay. But David's favorite way to make a sculpture is to use metal and fire. This is called **welding** (WEL-ding). David likes to work with metal because it is so strong. It lasts a long time. Metal is less likely to break than plaster or clay.

◄ David looks forward to creating new works of art in his studio on the weekends.

Making a Picture

David likes to start his day by playing music on the radio. He says this makes him feel ready to work. His dog, Pharro, keeps him company. Before David can make a sculpture, he draws a picture, or **sketch** (SKECH), of what he wants the sculpture to look like. This sketch can be the same size or smaller than the sculpture will be when it is finished. David cuts out the picture and traces it to a piece of metal.

Making sketches helps David plan his sculpture. ▶

Being Safe

Before David does anything else, he puts on some **protective** (proh-TEK-tiv) clothing. Sturdy boots protect his feet from heavy pieces of metal that might fall on his toes. When he works with a torch, he also wears special clothes to protect himself from being burned. Jeans cover his legs, and an apron keeps his body safe. He wears fireproof gloves so he won't burn his hands. He also puts on a face **shield** (SHEELD).

◀ David sculpts only after he has put on all of his protective clothes.

The Beginning of a Sea Horse

Today, David is making a sea horse sculpture. He puts the sketch of the sea horse on a big piece of metal. Then he uses white spray paint to paint around the edges. When he lifts off the paper, a perfect **outline** (OWT-lyn) is on the steel.

David is ready to cut out the sea horse. He pulls his face shield over his face, and Pharro gets out of the way. David and Pharro have to be very careful.

Using a sketch as his guide means that when David cuts out his sea horse, he won't waste any metal. ▶

Fire Cuts Metal

David turns on his cutting torch. A flame comes out of it. He puts the flame to the metal. Suddenly, sparks fly all around. It looks like the Fourth of July! Every once in a while there is a loud popping sound as David carefully follows the outline with the torch. The flame is cutting the metal! When it's done, the cutout of the sea horse falls to the floor with a loud crash. David can use the leftover metal another day for another project.

◀ David's cutting torch makes
sparks fly!

Cooling the Sea Horse

David turns off the flame. He carefully lifts the sea horse. Thick gloves protect David's hands so he doesn't feel the hot metal. He looks at the sea horse to make sure everything is right. Then he dips it into a bucket of water so it can cool. The metal is still so hot that the water starts to boil! Steam rises and the metal sizzles.

Next David takes the sea horse back to the welding table. He's not done yet. David turns on the flame again and begins to make an eye on the sea horse's face.

It's important to cool the metal in water right away so that David doesn't burn himself. ▶

The Sea Horse Gets a Twist

David wants to bend the metal a little bit to give the sea horse's tail a twist. He heats the metal once more. While he keeps the tail hot, he uses a wrench to twist it. The sea horse goes back into the bucket of water to cool. David is done cutting the sea horse.

David takes a thin pole and measures it. Then he cuts the pole quickly with the torch. David makes this into a base for his sculpture by welding it onto the sea horse. Now the sea horse can stand by itself.

◀ When you sculpt with metal, you need to be just as good at using tools as you are at coming up with ideas.

David's Favorite Part

David's favorite part is next. He will add **designs** (dih-ZYNZ) to the sea horse. He uses chalk to mark off scales on the sea horse's head and back. He uses a different torch to carve the designs in the sea horse.

This torch is electric. It has enough power in it to light up a house! David has to wear a special helmet with a face shield. The helmet protects his eyes and face from the heat. Wearing a shield makes the room look very dark.

David gets to be very creative as he adds designs to the sea horse. ▶

Signing His Work

Suddenly, in the dark room, David's lit torch shines brightly and the sea horse can be seen. The room gets smoky. Before David finishes his sculpture, he welds his **signature** (SIG-nuh-cher) and the date onto the sculpture. "It's really important for artists to sign their work," he says. "That way people will know who made it." Sometimes David paints his sculptures with bright colors or welds other shapes onto them. But this sculpture is done. David cleans up and starts another project.

◀ David is proud of all of his sculptures, big and small.

A Collection of Sculptures

David has made more than 300 sculptures. He sells most of his work to **museums** (myoo-ZEE-umz) and to people who like to collect it. Once a year David **exhibits** (eg-ZIH-bits) his art. People come from all over to look at his work and to buy his sculptures. David says he is happiest when he is working with his hands and being creative. "There are no rules to art," he says, "so you're free to do what you want. I think that's fun."

Glossary

design (dih-ZYN) A decoration on something.

exhibit (eg-ZIH-bit) A show put on for all people to see.

museum (myoo-ZEE-um) A building or rooms where a collection of objects is kept for people to see.

outline (OWT-lyn) A line drawn around the outer edges of something that shows its shape.

plaster (PLAS-ter) A soft mixture of sand, water and a mineral called lime, that hardens as it dries.

protective (proh-TEK-tiv) When something keeps you from harm.

sculptor (SKULP-ter) An artist who makes figures or objects using fire, wood, plaster, or other materials.

sculpture (SKULP-sher) A figure or object that is carved or formed.

shield (SHEELD) Something that protects a person from flying objects or bright lights.

signature (SIG-nuh-cher) A name of a person written in that person's own writing.

sketch (SKECH) A quick drawing.

studio (STOO-dee-oh) A room or building where an artist works.

welding (WEL-ding) Using heat to melt pieces of metal together.

Index